miniature gardens
in bowl, dish, and tray

miniature gardens
in bowl, dish, and tray

JACK KRAMER

Drawings by Cyrus Choy and James Carew

Charles Scribner's Sons, New York

Copyright © 1975 JACK KRAMER

Library of Congress Cataloging in Publication Data

Kramer, Jack, 1927-
    Miniature gardens in bowl, dish, and tray.

    Includes index.
    1. Gardens, Miniature.   I. Title.
SB419.K715   635.9'8   74-34007
ISBN 0-684-14301-1 (Cloth)
ISBN 0-684-14299-6 (Paper)

1 3 5 7 9 11 13 15 17 19 MD/C 20 18 16 14 12 10 8 6 4 2
1 3 5 7 9 11 13 15 17 19 M/P 20 18 16 14 12 10 8 6 4 2

Printed in the United States of America

Drawings in Chapters 1-7 by James Carew,
Chapters 8-21 by Cyrus Choy

contents

introduction:
nature at your fingertips

Green plants and colorful flowers, lush grasses and verdant mosses, are lovely additions to everyday life. Yet many people are unable to have them. They may be apartment dwellers, they may not have time nor strength to do extensive gardening nor have the money for it.

Now, there is an easy way to have nature at your fingertips without excessive cost, time, or effort. Everyone from eight to eighty can make miniature gardens in tray, bowl, or dish. Here, in lilliputian scale, you can have your garden and have as much satisfaction from it as from an outdoor garden. These small greeneries are not only for the eye, but for the soul as well.

Dish gardens have been with us for years but in all that time have been an assemblage of plants in any container, rather than a landscape scene. In this book, using the principles of bonkei and bonsai adapted to our culture, we bring the dish garden into its own as a miniature landscape and as a gardening art.

What we are doing is taking a segment of nature and refining it. In these small gardens we can remember a childhood walk through a woodland, a favorite desert scene which has stayed in the mind's eye, or you can create a rocky ledge landscape or a seacoast scene, a meadow garden, or almost any landscape you admire. It is fun to make tiny hills and mountains, to simulate lakes and streams, paths and walks. You are the artist painting the picture, the sculptor shaping the terrain, and the gardener growing the plants.

Nature is at your fingertips in these miniature gardens in bowl, dish, or tray.

JACK KRAMER

1 MINIATURE GARDENS

The small dish garden has been popular for many years. I remember my grandmother growing tiny plants in discarded household containers —bowls and trays. Her gardens showed care and love because she took time with every detail. Plants predominated in her miniature arrangements, but small figurines and little buildings were also included. She was in essence duplicating scenes from nature to decorate the indoors during the dull winter months in Chicago. As a table centerpiece or on a coffee table or mantel they were a unique decoration (some were actually model landscapes). On the other hand, the dish gardens I remember in florist stores in the 1940s were hardly as beautiful or as well-done as those of my grandmother; they were simply a hodgepodge of different plants in a dish or tray. Some were attractive, but the majority left a great deal to be desired.

This miniature tropical garden in a bowl is a complete scene in itself, a tiny piece of nature recreated in a container. Rocks are carefully selected and placed to provide a balanced landscape and plants judiciously placed—dracaena, peperomia and cordyline the accent plant. Small buildings and figures complete this handsome landscape. *(Photo by Matthew Barr)*

Dish gardens of the 1940s were haphazardly put together; merely a conglomerate of plants with no attention to creating a landscape. The result is an unattractive picture. *(Photo by Hort Pix)*

Just where or how the dish garden—a group of plants in a container—started I do not know. I have found it is far more gratifying to create a miniature garden with care and an eye to detail. They become works of art rather than assemblages of plants and can be truly beautiful. This book combines the art of the miniature garden and the principles of Japanese bonkei and sakei, that is, creating model landscapes; this marriage of East and West can provide many pleasant hours for you. While they can be called dish gardens or model landscapes, more technically they are miniature gardens which simulate natural scenes.

5

This tray landscape is simple but elegant with a single tree, grasses, and baby's tears. The tree is attached to the rock and both vertical and horizontal lines are given full consideration. *(Photo by Matthew Barr)*

6

CONSIDER THE GARDEN

Your lilliputian garden can be almost any landscape scene which appeals to you. You create the picture, and, although nature dictates what goes into it, it is still a personalized picture. You plant the trees, make the lakes or streams, sculpt the hills, lay the stone paths, and build the structures (houses and bridges). This is a garden and a decorative accent as well.

A miniature garden is a *complete whole in itself*. It is not something to do quickly or haphazardly; you should do it with pleasure and patience. Each detail counts, each blade of grass is important, and if first attempts seem less than perfect, try again. Eventually you will become proficient in making lilliputian landscapes. And do not forget that you are dealing with gardening as well as a craft.

For decorative beauty throughout the home, small gardens please the eye and soul. They can be used as accents on a windowsill or coffee table, in the kitchen or bathroom—any room in the home—and can be placed outdoors in summer to beautify patios and terraces. And they will forever provoke complimentary comments from friends.

There are vast rewards in this kind of gardening and it is yet another way that plants can add pleasure to your daily living. These gardens not only keep the mind working, they keep the fingers going.

SELECTING THEMES

It is not necessary, at first, to cope with grand designs. Try a simple landscape such as a house by a lake, or a woodland or a desert scene. Pick a theme which will not defeat you. Later you can go forward with waterfalls, streams, and hills, which, when properly made, are truly

A woodland garden with tiny ferns and acorus; small rocks are in the background and the grassy acorus is the accent plant bordered with *peperomia caperata*. Ground cover, sand, and gravel complete the miniature garden in a terra cotta container. *(Photo by author)*

works of art. (Miniature landscape themes and the plants are fully discussed in Chapter 6.)

Although you may prefer to work with live plants and mosses, artificial trees and shrubs can be used (but sparingly), provided they are made with an eye to detail. Like scale-model railroading, tiny structures should be perfect in every detail.

A desert scene is one of the easiest small gardens to assemble: a few plants, some well-chosen stones, and driftwood are all that is necessary to bring the desert indoors. The landscape is sparse, but therein is its beauty. Use sands of varying colors to denote land gradation. Select appropriate containers; the shallow matte brown bonsai dish is ideal because the curve of the bowl is more in keeping with the globe or barrel shapes of desert plants.

If the woodland is your favorite landscape, by all means duplicate this in miniature. In this scene there are many plants of many heights, and luxuriant mosses clothe the ground. Try to simulate a small water area; put in a handcrafted bridge to provide the illusion of reality. This garden is rarely level; it is hilly. A rectangular dish is the best container for the woodland scene.

A hillside scene, a house by a lake, or a river in a mountain are other beautiful landscapes for garden subjects. Think of scenes or settings you remember from nature which left an impression on you. Or, if you have a short memory, work from a photograph. If you like to do watercolors or sketches, copy these settings for your miniature gardens.

COMPOSITION AND DESIGN

Composition is the placement of trees and shrubs, grasses and mosses, structures and rivers, sand and gravel, soil and pebbles within the garden. Remember that in tiny gardens you are trying to recreate the grandeur of nature in the confines of a small tray; thus, the principle called illusion of distance must be used. This may seem like a secret, but actually it is merely making clear distinctions between near, middle, and distant objects or areas. In some cases using less rather than more will accomplish this end too—that is, part of the tray is left level without vegetation.

In a wooden tray with a galvanized metal liner, a simple meadow scene is recreated from nature. Ferns and acorus are the dominant plants and ground covers clothe the soil. *(Photo by author)*

Another element of successful miniature gardening involves selecting the right plant to suggest the tree or shrub you wish to duplicate. Small boxwoods with woody stems make ideal trees, as do some miniature begonias. Malpighia, podocarpus, and a host of other house plants suggest trees to the trained eye. For true bonsai trees use *Picea conica glauca, Chamaecyparis pisifera*, and the many Zelkovas.

Lush forests can be simulated by using ground covers such as dwarf baby's tears (*Helxine nana*), Selaginella, small peperomias, and Irish moss. Trailing plants are especially graceful cascading over sculptured mountains, and do not forget ferns, which add charm to any scene. The palette is limitless once you get your imagination started.

Within the three-area design allow one area to predominate; it will be the focal point of the garden. It may be on the left or right side of the tray, front or rear, but never in the center. Anything that divides the garden will ruin total harmony, which is paramount in small gardens. Even the incorrect placement of a pebble can destroy a scene. Everything must be *just right*. If this sounds foolish, remember how you arranged your living room furnishings; a table too close to a sofa or a chair in the wrong place destroys the total picture.

Desert gardens in miniature are always handsome and this one uses sedums and echeverias in a shallow clay tapered bowl. The arrangement is pleasing, plants compatible and a total landscape is created. *(Photo by Hort Pix)*

Mountains and hills are integral parts of nature and always eye-appealing. In miniature gardens they are stellar subjects. Sometimes you may be lucky, and a rock or stone you find may suggest a hill. Other times you can use modeling clay to make the mountain. Valleys and ledges are other appealing parts of natural landscapes. Small pieces of slate, one on top of the other, can be made to look like ledges, as can pieces of clay pots if handled properly. Use your imagination. Visualize. Design and create. Beautiful rivers and streams can also be recreated in gardens; use sand, gravel, and pebbles. But there is a little more to it than that. Sand must be the right grade and color, and all materials must be placed just right to fool the eye from a distance.

All this may seem like magic, but it need not be once you have mastered the art of using the proper plants and materials in their proper places. And in the following chapters we show and tell you how to do it!

2 tools and basic materials

Having basic inexpensive tools on hand when you need them can mean the difference between an ordinary miniature garden and an extraordinary one. All you need for the ordinary dish garden are the container, soil, and plants, but the model landscape or miniature garden requires several basic helpers to fashion the details in the garden—it is the details that make the garden splendid. Besides soil and plants and some tools, basic materials such as wires, rocks, sand, and pebbles are the finishing touches to your imaginative creations. They add the natural garnish to make a landscape alive rather than just a conglomeration of plants in soil in a container.

Through the years I have accumulated odds and ends, various tools I have made myself or found in kitchen stores. Because these tools helped me so much I will talk about them here to help you create your miniature gardens.

BASIC TOOLS

Small manicure scissors should perhaps be the first tool because you can trim and prune the smallest plant so that it fits into the land-scape as you want it to appear: a small tree, a bush, a hedge. You should also have a pair of standard scissors for cutting wires and roots. A small garden shears, or, better yet, a bonsai pincettes, which is pointed, is excellent for trimming woody plants; this tool can also be used for loosening soil from old pots and scraping down soil.

Another tool I rely on is a small pocketknife for cutting and pruning branches. You can get angle cuts with the knife, and usually branches and stems should be cut at an angle rather than straight across. For very fine detail, such as the pruning and shaving of barks and stems, I use a single-edged razor blade.

A trowel is also necessary. Search for the very small ones, or if pressed, use a small sugar scoop (found at kitchen stores). A trowel is for repotting and digging into soil. Bamboo chopsticks are also handy for loosening old soil and tamping down new soil around plant roots. Pliers are needed for fashioning wire in training some plants, and use a small hammer for tapping and breaking rocks or pots. You will also want some fine mesh hardware cloth to cover drain holes in pots.

Copper wires of various gauges are necessary for fixing and attaching rocks, stones, and plants and for training branches and stems to

Gravel, rocks, stone, are all part of the miniature landscape; tools include knife, shears, and the container is a shallow bonkei dish. *(Photo by author)*

various designs. You can use florist wire (already cut in convenient lengths), or buy wire by the spool and cut your own lengths. Friction tape or paper tape for wrapping stems and branches is also a good idea. Animal hair brushes for cleaning fragile leaves are also necessary. Select several brushes of different sizes; you will need more than one, I assure you, to create really fine landscapes.

You will need two various-sized sprayers for watering: one with a fine mist, the other to deliver a slightly more coarse mist. String for tying and holding plants in place is also a good idea, and, finally, you might want to have some sieves for mixing your soils.

15

ROCKS AND PEBBLES

If you want beautiful model landscapes, you will have to use rocks of all sizes because they add great interest and eye appeal. You can, of course, collect rocks yourself from streams, roadsides, or wherever, or you can buy them from suppliers. Pebbles smaller than rocks are also necessary to add dimension and contrast to the tiny gardens. These come in all shapes and sizes too.

Although rocks measuring from 2 to 6 inches in height are used mostly for landscaping, you might also want to try flat shale to build up charming terraces and ledges. Set the shales on top of each other at

Rocks come in all shapes and sizes—vertical and horizontal. Selecting the right rocks for a landscape is an integral part of good design. Osmunda forms the base to hold rocks in place and is wired through drainage holes in tray. *(Photo by author)*

varying levels, and fasten them to each other with waterproof epoxy or clay.

The shapes of rocks are infinite, resembling waterfalls, statues, tunnels, hills, escarpments, stalagmites, and so on. There is a world of shapes and contours to play with, governed only by your imagination. Colors vary too, from deep dusky reds to shiny black to granite grays to winter green and almost any color in between. (The arrangement of rocks is fully covered in Chapter 5.)

The oval-shaped, smooth, and rounded cobblestones in white or black, especially handsome, are yet another "prop" for gardens. I purchase them at various florists. They come in two finishes, satiny smooth or natural, and are excellent for meandering paths and small accent areas, where they circle little grasses and perhaps diminutive violets. Also use some large jagged stones with rough surfaces in infinite shapes to delight the eye and provide contrast.

SANDS AND GRAVELS

These materials are indispensable to the dish gardener because they are the finishing touches. There is more to sand than just sand: it comes in several colors and in several sizes. What you want is small-sieved sand or very fine granules, *not* pebbles. Sand is vital for foundations and top decorations, so do not buy just any kind. Colors range from brownish white to white to black or blue. You will find the black-brown-white sand, which is used as a planting base in aquariums, at tropical-fish suppliers, but the finely sieved colored sand may take some searching for.

Gravel (crushed pebbles) is larger in size than sand and may be used in conjunction with sand to give dimension to a landscape. Gravel is white, brown, or black, and it can be used alone for decoration and paths or with sand to vary the interest. It is also useful for propping rocks at angles.

SOILS

Along with sands and gravel, rocks and pebbles, soil for plants to grow in and take nourishment from is a vital part of successful tray gardening. Potted plants can live in regular packaged soil, but the soil for little gardens should be hand-mixed. The soil should contain no fertilizers, drain well, and be granular in form. Most packaged soils are simply too heavy. The soil you want must have spaces between the grains to allow water and air to reach plant roots easily; this kind of soil will produce lush healthy plants.

To get the best soil medium, sift soil through a large meshed ½-inch sieve. Take some of the soil that falls through the ½-inch sieve and sift it through a ¼-inch sieve; take some of this soil in turn and sift it through a 1/16-inch sieve. You now have three grades of soil. Mix these together for the final medium. Always keep soil dry because wet or moist soil is impossible to work with.

Rich soil is mixed with sand in preparation for planting. *(Photo by USDA)*

Soil is put through a sieve and will be sieved again before ready for planting. *(Photo by USDA)*

OSMUNDA

This is a material for potting orchids, but it serves equally as well for fashioning hills and foundations for model landscapes. Osmunda is the fibrous root of two types of osmunda fern and resembles spongy wire. It holds water (but not too much) and dries out slowly over a period of time. The material also has spaces between the fiber to allow circulation of air. As osmunda decays, usually in 2 or 3 years, it releases nutrients for plant growth. Osmunda is available in packages (from orchid dealers) in large chunks about a foot square. It can be cut or pulled apart by hand and is easy to use to make hills and foundations because you can control the size you want (unlike a rock or stone, which generally must be used as is).

19

Attaching wires through drainage holes in tray to hold osmunda and rocks in place. *(Photo by author)*

Osmunda is inexpensive and steamed; thus it does not promote disease organisms or attract insects. Because it bears some resemblance to peat moss, suppliers may tell you to substitute peat, but do not do it—peat moss is an entirely different product.

SPHAGNUM

Sphagnum, another building base for tray landscapes, is sold in sacks at nurseries. Sphagnum is a light elastic material somewhat like osmunda but not as compact. It is somewhat feathery and falls apart easily. Although it is not as easy to use as osmunda, in some cases sphagnum is satisfactory. When you ask for sphagnum, specify the live kind because there is an artificial type which is not good at all for surfacing miniature gardens.

Sphagnum is the basic building material here along with rocks to establish a landscape scene. Only a few plants are used: orchids and a zygocactus. *(Photo by Matthew Barr)*

MOSSES

Moss adds an authentic touch to tray landscapes, and soil clothed in green always is lovely to look at. Moss also conserves moisture and is a good indicator of the condition of the soil: when the moss is somewhat brittle and brown, the soil beneath needs watering. Green moss indicates that the moisture of the soil is fine.

You will find it almost impossible to buy true mosses, so generally you will have to grow your own by collecting it in nature. Moss

To plant a miniature garden, first put gravel and charcoal chips in place; add some pot shards. *(Photo by author)*

Here, planting holes have been dug and plants put in place and soil pushed around collar of plants. Note handsome cobblestones as a decoration. *(Photo by author)*

grows in damp areas which receive little light, and in early spring you will find it in your garden on the shady sides of tree trunks and stones. To collect it, slide a blade under the moss, taking some soil with it, and lift it in pieces as you would slice a layer cake. Keep the moss moist until it is ready for planting in your lilliputian garden. Once it is ready, take the slices and dry them on newspaper or cardboard. Remove the green part of the moss by crumbling away the soil. The fine-dried moss will be your "starter" for your own crop. Make a soil-and-peat mixture in a shallow tray (use any household item such as a milk carton cut lengthwise or an aluminum dish that frozen rolls come in). Insert a layer of cheesecloth over the soil, and now sprinkle the dried moss on top. Cover this with another layer of cheesecloth, and water lightly but thoroughly with a fine mist. Put the moss in a shady place, with temperature about 75° to 80°F. In about 2 months moss should start growing and in another month will be ready for use in your tray gardens.

There are so many wild mosses it would be impossible to name them all, but some of the best for tray gardening are *Bryum argenteum*, *Pholia camptotrachtera*, and *Hynum plumaeforme*. Available from bonsai suppliers is a packaged product called Kyoto moss. The seed can be planted anytime during the year; treat it in the same way as you would wild moss.

The completed miniature garden with a miniature orchid, *peperomia caperata*, and gravel and sand. *(Photo by author)*

GRASSES AND GROUND COVERS

It may seem strange to include grasses in the accessory chapter rather than in the plant section, but like mosses, grasses are the finishing touches to a tray miniature. Grasses include such plants as miniature bamboo (*Bambusa nana*), small Sasa plants, and Arundinaria (the small ones). Use these lovely leafy plants to fill in between rocks and stones or as groves themselves to simulate a meadow. Ordinary grass seed can also be used; sprinkle a few seeds in the soil of the model landscape; when they start growing, trim and manicure the grass to your liking. With grass, simply slice a portion of it with the soil intact and insert it into the landscape.

Ground covers, which many people use as a substitute for the hard-to-find mosses, are also excellent finishing touches for the miniature garden. Generally, these plants include Scotch moss, Irish moss, baby's tears, Camomile, and tiny sedums. These plants spread rapidly and will need frequent trimming to keep them in bounds and attractive. Yet they are readily available and can certainly be used.

FIGURINES AND ORNAMENTS

When most people think of figurines, they think of garish plastic "statues." These are *not* the ones we talk about here. The figurines for tray landscapes should be finely made, with a detail for reality. Look for balsa wood or ceramic figures and ornaments, generally sold at bonsai dealers.

The ornaments may be human figures or buildings or animals and are made in perfect scale to match your tray-garden landscapes. Use ornaments and figurines with discretion: too many will defeat the pur-

Figurines

COUNTRY BRIDGE

STEPS

① DECK
2"x 1"

② BASE POSTS
½"x ½"

③ SIDE BOARD
2"x ¼"

④ POSTS
1¼"x ¼"

MATERIALS

Balsa wood- 4", 2", ½" and ¼".

Elmer's glue

Ex-acto knife

⑤ RAIL GUARD
2"x ¼"

⑥ RAIL POSTS
¾"x ¼"

⑦ POST BRACE
1"x ¼"

⑧ ROOF
2¼"x 1
Leave 1/16"excess -
overlap this when
gluing

pose, but one finely crafted miniature house or bridge can be very handsome in the proper setting.

If commercial "props" do not fit your needs or tastes, you can fashion small bridges and model-scale houses on your own. By using thin balsa wood and modern epoxies you can build many unique and beautiful structures for your miniature landscapes. A pattern on paper is essential; cut out pieces according to the specifications and glue them together. This is not only a way of having very fine accompaniments to your gardens but is also a fascinating hobby. (It is somewhat like putting together model airplanes.) And you have the satisfaction of knowing you have distinctive pieces for your garden.

CLAYLIKE MATERIALS

In Japanese bonkei a claylike material called *Keto* peat is used to fashion small hills and mountains. This material is difficult to find in the United States, but you can use powdered asbestos mixed with water to fashion land contours. This material is used by plumbers to protect pipes and ducts and is available and inexpensive. When moistened it becomes like clay and can easily be molded into various shapes. The asbestos is gray so I sprinkle it with soil or colored gravel to create a more realistic effect.

Papier mâché is sometimes suggested for molding hills and valleys but this is not practical for our purposes. Being made of paper it is easily destroyed by excess moisture and, although it is possible to keep water away from the specific papier mâché areas, this is tedious.

3 containers for miniature gardens

The container for a miniature garden is more than just something to grow plants in; it is as important as the plants you are putting into it. As with bonsai, the container and plants should complement each other and create a total scene. But the container for a model landscape can and should match the plants, either in motif, lines, shape, or design.

Finding just the right container for your small plants is fun; it makes for pleasurable rummaging in salvage shops and kitchen boutiques. The tray, dish, bowl—you name it—may be wood or bronze,

Containers

china or glass, or ceramic. Ironically, you will not find many of these in the usual line of containers for plants. The most original containers are those that are made for entirely different purposes. For example, pottery dishes of diminutive green plants are stunning, and even the smallest teacup or ashtray can become a unique model landscape with the right plants. Bonsai and sakei trays offer yet another array of beautiful containers for your miniature plants, and natural housings such as gourds and rocks, pieces of wood, and seashells are other fine possibilities.

CONTAINERS YOU BUY

You will find these in stores which sell plant supplies. A store-bought container can be simply a terra cotta, deep, clay saucer; a tapered terra cotta pot; one of the squat azalea pots that measure only 3 or 4 inches in depth; and so on. A terra cotta saucer measures 1 or 2 inches in depth and thus calls for really low-growing hip-hugging plants. A low hilly terrain in miniature will complement the saucer, and plants such as sedums and tiny-leaved ivy will be very suitable.

The tapered terra cotta pot measures 4 to 5 inches in depth. This container requires somewhat taller plants, with a center-of-interest plant. Here, too, the contour of the soil should be mounded, with one high hill and lesser hills. Leaves can be medium-sized from 1 to 2 inches, or very small, such as Muhlenbeckia, which has a ¼-inch leaf. Because the dish is cone-shaped, the terrain too should be in an inverted cone shape to balance the setting. Place plants accordingly, with the small ones at the perimeter, graduating to large ones at the top, with an accent plant which is slightly taller than the others.

The azalea pot demands a more flat terrain. Some small cascading ground covers to cover the pot edges will soften the setting, although plants of all kinds can be used. However, no plant should be taller than,

An oval tray of rich brown color is a container for this grove scene. Note the hilly terrain and again, the use of ground covers and gravel. *(Photo by author)*

This container for a simple desert garden is a white china casserole. *(Photo by author)*

say, 10 inches. Interesting stones and gravel should be added to the landscape to create dimension in the scene.

Bonsai trays and dishes now come in a variety of shapes, sizes, and designs. The true sakei tray may be only 1 inch deep, amoeboid in shape, and very handsome and suitable for miniature landscapes. Bonsai dishes are standard height, that is, 4 to 6 inches in depth, in square, rectangular, octagonal, or hexagonal shapes (ovals and circles are available too). Many bonsai dishes also come with a tray, and it is a good idea to buy both tray and dish because it makes the scene complete. Sizes of bonsai containers may be from 2 to 14 inches across, so there is a wide variety; what you choose depends upon just how many plants and what kind of scene you want to create.

You will also find some in-between designs, generally rectangular vessels with rounded corners and flared sides. These are especially good for dish gardens, and, being 12 inches square, have ample room for almost any scene you want to make.

Colors of all these containers vary, but in the unglazed ones matte brown or bisque is popular, and in the glazed types blue is the favorite. White and black dishes are also frequently seen, but I have had difficulty in making attractive dish gardens in pure white dishes because the color is too stark and too sharp a contrast to the green of the plants.

OTHER-PURPOSE CONTAINERS

This catchall category includes teacups and goblets, liqueur glasses, butter tubs, soy kegs—you name it. There are hundreds, and what you choose is governed only by your imagination. Kitchen items too, such as casseroles, pottery, and dishes, make excellent ideas for containers. Generally these containers will be small and require only a few plants or perhaps just one, like a diminutive fern in a teacup. Model landscape scenes as such will probably be out of scale, but do look for choice plants. Tin cans, or for that matter any squatty can, may become a container for a greenery too. Coffee cans are especially good, and they are available in many sizes. You will have to paint the outside or cover it with Contact paper.

The idea is never to throw anything away without first thinking whether it could become a decorative item with a few plants. And as you shop at salvage stores, flea markets, or garage sales, keep your eyes open for that unique container which can become a home for your plants.

NATURAL CONTAINERS

Nature, forever with us, has seemed more prominent in recent years. For example, pots for plants are now being manufactured with

A shallow bonkei tray is used for this landscape where stones and gravel predominate. *(Photo by author)*

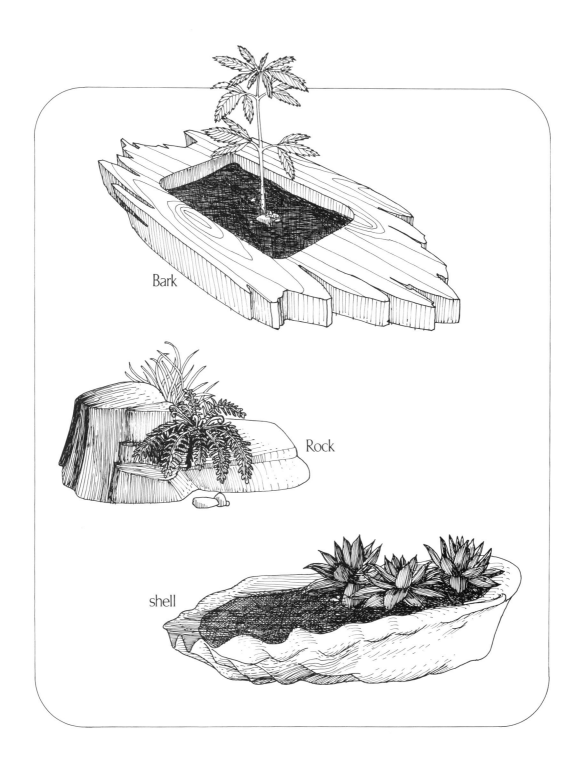

Bark

Rock

shell

Natural Containers

A natural rock with an eroded pocket is used for this miniature garden scene. In time the plants—mainly small sedums—will cover the rock. *(Photo by Joyce R. Wilson)*

exteriors that look like tree bark and cork. But do avoid those simulated containers because once you get plants in them they look worse than they do without greenery: the beautiful plants only emphasize the phoniness of the container. On the other hand, do watch for real pieces of tree bark, cactus skeletons, and such which can become beautiful settings for plants. Driftwood too is certainly appropriate for these lilliputian scenes.

Gourds in all sizes are sold at some boutique places, and, if they are cleverly planted, they are quite suitable for plants. (Generally these will be hanging gardens which can do much to bring beauty to a room.)

Large stones or rocks with natural eroded pockets are also very satisfactory for plants, and I have seen many handsome succulent collections growing in such natural surroundings with great flair. Large conches and seashells can also be used, provided you select appropriate plants and use good design in arranging them.

CONCRETE CONTAINERS

Gardening on a miniature scale in small troughs, sinks, or trays is popular in England. A stone sink garden can be quite handsome, brimming with tiny plants. Unfortunately, finding these containers is very difficult, but occasionally they show up in salvage shops. Old porcelain sinks can be used too, if you can find them. Actually, any concrete or porcelain housing 4 to 6 inches deep is fine. And you can always make your own concrete containers because it is not difficult.

Whatever salvageable or do-it-yourself container you have, be sure there are drainage holes in the bottom so excess water can escape. To plant a small garden, cover the bottom of the container with a ½-inch layer of tiny stones. Add some charcoal chips; then put in soil to about ⅓ the depth of the container. Press the soil in place to eliminate air pockets, and then start shaping the landscape to make it ready for the plants (see the next chapter). A stone tray garden filled with soil is heavy, so assemble it where it will be permanently placed, preferably where there is some sunlight during the day.

To make a concrete tray or trough you will need wood framing for the forms, built to the size you want. The concrete mix should be fairly stiff: 3 parts cement, 1 part sand, and 2 parts pebbles. (Or use commercial concrete mixes and add water.) Pour the mix into the forms, put a presoaked standard clay pot in position, and fill in and around it with concrete to the top of the frame. Twenty-four hours later strip off the wood form and remove the pot. Run water over the surface, and then scrub the surface with a wire brush.

You can also make a concrete container by using two cardboard boxes or cartons. One should be small enough to leave 1½ or 2 inches of space at the bottom and four sides when placed inside the other carton. Pour 2 inches of concrete mix into the first carton. Tamp down with a wooden stick, and then put the smaller carton inside. Pour and tamp mix in between the two cartons to make the wall of the container. Cardboard forms can be removed in a day. Let the concrete dry for a few days, and then shape it to the desired form with a chisel. Scrub the container with a wire brush, and then wet it down several times. It is now ready for soil and miniature plants for your model landscape.

A very handsome arrangement of sempervivums are right at home in this handsome stone container, an exquisite landscape garden. *(Photo by Roy Elliot)*

4 design and planting

With terrariums you are restricted to certain heights for plants, but the dish garden has no limitation. Also, strict forms such as upright or round do not have to be observed because there are no glass or plastic sides to thwart growth. So even though the planning of a dish garden may seem similar to a terrarium planting, there are vast differences. And because there is an infinite choice of containers, the dish garden offers a wider scope of miniature scenes than the close confines of the terrarium.

The arrangement you create should depict a scene from nature

Top: Soil, gravel, sand, and stones, along with miniature cacti wait for their new home. These few plants are all that is needed to create a handsome desert landscape. *Middle*: A barrel cactus being taken from pot to be planted in the sandy soil base. *Bottom*: Plants and rocks are in place and now sand is spooned to create an interesting terrain. *(Photos by author)*

but in miniature; a dish garden should be an artistic endeavor as well as a unique way of growing indoor plants. It should never be simply a group of plants in a container. As mentioned previously, think of scenes you have seen in nature: a woodland path, a hilly nook, a secluded valley. Let your imagination roam. Perhaps use a photograph as a guide. You can assemble the garden as you go along, but a quick sketch on paper can help you pull all the elements—rocks, stones, plants, soil—together.

DRAW IT ON PAPER

You do not have to be an artist to draw on paper; simply sketch in forms of trees, shrubs, mosses, and rocks and pebbles. Even a simple drawing will tell you something about proportion, balance, and harmony, which are the basic parts of an attractive small landscape scene. For example, draw in a small treelike plant such as *Punica nana* (pomegranate) as a focal point and work around that, or perhaps try a group of low-growing peperomias in one corner as a start. Group small plants rather than isolating one here or there, giving a spotty effect.

For square or rectangular containers the plant arrangement will differ from a garden in an oval or circular tray. Draw and redraw until shapes balance each other, until there is proportion and harmony and the garden takes on a character, whether it be a mountain stream scene, a desert landscape, or a tropical rain forest.

DESIGNING THE GARDEN

Once you have a suitable drawing, start to create your visual picture in real life with appropriate plants. Have all material on hand at the start—container, soil, gravel, rocks, pieces of wood, and plants. If you are using a rectangular tray, start in the rear corner and create small hills, making dramatic use of line and rhythm combined with color texture and structural forms. Verticals should be balanced with horizontals, and there should be unity throughout. To construct the corner arrangement, use small pieces of flat slate or shale; even broken pieces of clay pots will do. Set these pieces in layers on a small bed of soil, one on top of the other, and then cover the projection with sphagnum. Leave the edges of the slate or pot pieces showing here and there to simulate a natural rock outcropping. Balance the one rock mass with a smaller group of pebbles on the left side of the container but somewhat further from the edge than the right-hand vertical accent. Place plants in place with regard for height. Use either a group of plants all the same height or a group with varying heights, such as three medium growers, three tall ones, and three short ones. On the right side use taller plants, and in between the arc plant low growers, that is, creepers and trailers and perhaps mosses to clothe the soil.

If you use round or oval containers, once again install a somewhat hilly terrain or one large hill and a slightly undulating terrain for the rest of the scene. Build islands of rock or wood, with plants slightly to the left or right. Generally in an oval or round container one island is all that is necessary. Smaller ground cover plants placed in an arc will create balance and harmony.

The following principles govern the design of the garden, although gardens may be of many different themes:

1. Materials like rocks, pebbles, or gravel should be repeated more than twice so there is harmony in the garden.
2. Although you want many plants, do not create a jungle; use restraint and good taste.
3. Make all parts of the design in pleasing proportion.
4. Be sure the container itself is in character with the landscape you create.
5. Select one theme, such as formal or informal, natural or simple, and stick to it.

1. Insert gravel or shards; add soil

2. Shape contour of soil; add rocks

3. Place plants near rocks; firm soil around collar

4. The planted landscape

Potting Tray Landscape

1. Insert stones for drainage
2. Add soil
3. Place plant
4. Cross section: soil / sand / gravel

Cross Section: Tray Landscape

Top: Screens are placed over the drainage holes of the tray and gravel is set in place to facilitate drainage, in readiness to planting the garden. *Bottom*: Soil has been placed in the container and a small evergreen tree is being pruned at the roots before planting. (*Photos by author*)

46

PUTTING IT TOGETHER

Over the drain holes of a clean container, lay in pieces of mesh screen so soil will not sift out. Now add a thin layer of pea gravel with some charcoal chips to keep the soil sweet. Put a layer of rich soil (see Chapter 2, the section on soil) to within ½ inch of the top of the tray. Now start to create your landscape by placing rocks in place. Some rocks, if they are heavy, can stand by themselves, but others may have to be wired in place. To do this, insert florists' wire around the rocks and through the drainage holes, tying them together. Take your time and be true to nature. Make rock croppings and hills appear natural. Use pieces of wood bark and such with discretion. A single chunk of wood will look just like that. Embed the wood in the soil; use smaller

Violets are put in place in the miniature landscape and soil pushed around collar of the plant. (*Photo by author*)

pieces to accompany it and make it appear as though it has been there for years. This is easily done by covering the wood with soil or osmunda and then later adding appropriate mosses to clothe the scene (discussed in the next section).

If you have a flat tray, do not make the landscape flat; build it up with rock groupings and osmunda wired in place. Chunks of osmunda covered with sphagnum are easy to fashion and will create a dimension and visual interest in the garden.

Most plants will come in 2- or 3-inch pots in soil; remove the plants from their pots by tapping the pot against the edge of a table. Crumble away some of the soil from the root ball, and dig small holes in the soil for the plants. Place plants where you want them, and then firm the soil around the collar of the plant. Do not envelope the plant in soil or shallow-plant it. Put the soil around the collar of the plant, where it was originally in the pot.

Small grasses, stones, and ground covers have been planted and cobblestones pressed in soil for finishing touches to this tray garden. (*Photo by author*)

48

The finished tray garden with suitable props. (*Photo by author*)

As you arrange the garden, remember to use plants of different heights and different colors to create an attractive picture. Use dark greens next to medium greens next to pale greens. Never jump abruptly from a group of dark plants to pale green plants because this jars the eye. Also consider leaf size and texture. Larger-leaved plants should be next to medium-leaved plants and these, in turn, next to small-leaved plants so there is graduation in leaf size, never a sudden change from large to tiny leaves.

When the garden is all arranged, trim and prune plants so they have graceful lines and are not a jumble of stems and leaves. Removing a leaf here or there or a stem which obstructs a vista will not harm the plant; indeed, it will encourage it to grow. Line is vitally important to the whole picture. The plants must flow one into the other without abrupt voids. Remember that you are trying to create a scene from nature, and nature is a master craftsman.

FINISHING TOUCHES

When all plants and rocks are in place it is time to use what I call the frosting on the cake—pebbles and gravel and sand and mosses. The entire surface of the soil should be covered. This is the secret of an attractive miniature landscape scene. Place mosses at edges of plant groups and along the perimeter of stone and wood outcroppings. Get all mosses in place; at least ¼ of the soil surface should be covered with mosses or creeping plants. Now start adding islands of gravel. Use pea gravel of varying sizes: small, medium, and large. For the final touch lay brown, white, or black sand in place either in bare areas or along the edges of the gravel islands.

5 WORKING WITH PEBBLES AND ROCKS

When you fashion miniature gardens you will need more than soil and plants; rocks, pebbles, gravel, and sand are other important parts of a really handsome miniature garden. For simple definition, a rock is over 2 inches in diameter, 6 or 7 inches high. Pebbles are small rocks less than 2 inches in diameter, and gravel is crushed pebbles. Rocks, as previously mentioned, may be used as islands or ledges to create the landscape, or many times plants may be grown on rocks for a very realistic effect. Either way, using rocks as part of the garden is a fascinating procedure

The rocks used here simulate a ledge scene; the dominant plant is a mistletoe fig which appears as a giant tree and a maidenhair fern adds a graceful note. (*Photo by Matthew Barr*)

because it teaches us to truly appreciate the beauty of every rock and pebble and to look at our natural materials in a new light. Every rock you see takes on new interest as to whether it might be suitable for a little garden. And plants grown on rocks look handsome, much more natural than they sometimes do in soil because the rock gives dimension to the scene.

Selecting the right rocks, placing them correctly in the container, and adhering plants to them are what you must know to assemble the arrangement properly. Almost every rock has some merit and beauty, and you must learn to distinguish between the good and the not-so-good ones.

ROCKS

Any roadside rock can be used or, of course, you can purchase them at aquarium shops. The color, texture, and shape of the rock determine just how to use it. The rock may be flat on top, rounded, or perhaps coming to a point. It should, if possible, have a natural eroded pocket to receive the plant roots. Above all, it must have graceful lines and appear attractive. Try to use the best side of the rock because it always seems that one side is more handsome than the other. Let us look at nine rock shapes:

1. Slopes gracefully to one side.
2. Almost equal in all proportions, more like a large cobblestone.
3. Resembles a steep cliff.
4. Broad at the base and smaller at the top.
5. Triangular shaped.
6. Flat overall.
7. Smooth gentle slopes.
8. Upright.
9. Tunnel-like hollows.

These are just some of the shapes; others can be used too, depending upon what you find.

The more color within the rock, the better accent it will make; however, black or gray, white or bleached stones are dramatic too. The more contours, the more edges and crevices, the more interesting the stone will be.

The rock should be stable in the tray, so embed the bottom in a layer of soil and mound the soil over the base to be sure it is firm.

A small blue glazed bowl holds a diminutive desert scene. Two rocks flank the main cactus and smaller cacti, round in shape, are at the front and for contrast a rosette type Agave is at left. (*Photo by author*)

54

This handsome miniature garden could be in the middle of the forest. There is excellent proportion here between rocks and plants as well as a fine marriage of plant textures from broad leaves of the Ruellia plant to the graceful fronds to the tiny leaves of the ground cover. A small figurine in center adds dimension to the arrangement. (*Photo by Matthew Barr*)

PLANTING ON ROCKS

The plant you select should be in proportion to the size of the rock; it should not be too tall or too short—it must complement the rock (see Chapter 6 for plants). To start, attach some osmunda to the rock by cutting it into thin layers and placing it in position on the rock where the plant is to be placed. Firmly secure the osmunda with wires wrapped around the rock, or affix it with epoxy. (Use an epoxy which will not disintegrate in water.) To secure the plant in place you will need wire loops and a piece of lead (sold at bonsai suppliers). Make the loops from florists' wire, and secure the lead weight in the loop. Near where the plant is to be placed, chisel a small hole for the lead weight, keeping the wires of the loop extended so they can wrap around the collar of the plant. On the other side of the rock—that is, the side without the osmunda—again chisel a hole, put in a lead weight, and keep the wires extended. Now put the plant in position against the osmunda, and tie the four extended wires together. The plant must be firm against the osmunda so it can grow into it in time.

For the actual planting procedure, loosen the plant in its pot and tease it loose. Remove only as much of the root ball as necessary, and prune roots ever so lightly. Try the tree in several positions until you find the place where it looks best. Then proceed with the osmunda bed on the rock and affix the plant. Now fill the tray with soil, and complete the arrangement with other rock groups and gravel and sand according to the natural scene you have in mind.

We have given directions for the placing of one plant, but you can also use two or three plants on a rock, depending upon the size of the plants and the rock.

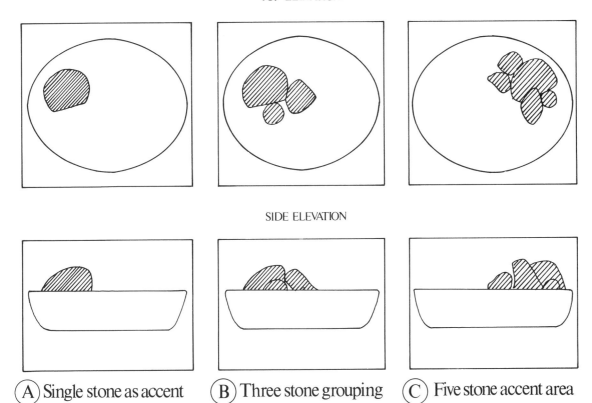

SIDE ELEVATION

(A) Single stone as accent   (B) Three stone grouping   (C) Five stone accent area

Rock Placement
for Tray Landscapes

A closeup of rock formation which provides the ledge of this landscape scene. Note how the rocks are embedded in the soil and how each stone has been placed in position. (*Photo by Matthew Barr*)

ROCK GROUPINGS

The plant on a rock will be an accent; you will want other groups of rocks to balance the miniature scene. Seek interesting smaller ones, not as large as the accent rock. Use one, three, five, or seven in a group, use the same kind to create a mass, rather than different rocks, which will create a spotty effect. Try to select rocks of similar shapes which naturally go together, but be sure they are of varying size because rocks of the same size give little or no depth. Also, different heights provide constant eye interest.

When you place one rock flat, all the rocks should be in the same position so each one relates to the other. The centers of the rocks should not be on the same line, and space should always be left on the side of the tray where the group is placed. (The direction of the rock is determined by the grooves in it.) When placing rocks, be sure that the center of the group is near the back of the container; this creates distance and illusion and makes the scene seem real. If you are using a single rock, position it a little in front of the center line of the tray.

By careful selection the rock grouping will balance the accent plant and rock on the other side. Now add soil to the tray landscape, mounding it up around the base of all rocks. Add small mosses and creepers in the spaces between to create a flow of plant material and give rhythm to the scene. Press soil down lightly with your thumbs so it is firm in the container, and water gradually and thoroughly from the outer edge of the container to the inward area. For finishing touches, you can embed small pebbles (1/4 inch in diameter) in islands here and there around the rock groups and add appropriately colored gravel and sand areas.

A closeup from a tray garden showing the beautiful use of textures of plants, rocks, sand, and gravel. (*Photo by Matthew Barr*)

60

6 plants and miniature landscape scenes

The plants you use for your model landscapes will be house plants (bonsai or sakei pieces are outdoor specimens). They will eventually grow into large plants, but for some time they are ideal in the small garden. (After they have outgrown the container you can remove them and use them as pot plants.) True miniatures like African violets, geraniums and begonias, and miniature orchids are the first choice for tray gardening. However, they are not generally sold at local nurseries, so you must order them from mail-order sources.

Ferns (*Photo by author*)

Terrarium plants, other good choices for model landscapes, include Selaginella, *Saxifraga sarmentosa*, peperomia, and Pileas. Cacti and succulents are fine for *desert* landscapes only; the shapes of most succulents, except for *Crassula argentea*, which looks like a tree, are not particularly suggestive of natural plants. And ferns and palms in their seedling state are perfect for little gardens, especially ferns like *Microlepia setosa* and *Camptosorus rhizophyllus*. Sago palms as babies are fine for dish gardens because they do impart a treelike effect. Other dwarf ferns and small palms can be used too.

All house plants have certain shapes or forms, and you should know the forms before you start the model landscape. It is far easier to follow a specific theme in your miniature landscapes and indeed more beautiful than to just put plants in a container. The type of small garden scene you create can be verdant woodland greenery complete with small trees and terrain; an oceanside picture, dramatic and unique; a country garden reminiscent of earlier days; and so on. Try to visualize what a plant simulates best—tree, bush, grass, shrub—because in each case specific landscapes demand specific shapes to make them look realistic.

Any scene you remember from nature can be duplicated in a tray, and after some experience it will appear like a miniature version of the real things. There are no sets of rules for developing each garden, but the following suggestions and recommended plants for each scene will help you start your own tiny landscapes.

COASTLINE GARDENS (Sea Coast, Rocky Ledge)

The beauty of the coastline garden, stark but dramatic, makes a suitable miniature tray scene. The formation of the landscape is of prime importance because appropriate small stones and rocks that simulate coastal formations must be selected. The process of creating this garden depends upon layering and stacking the stones to look like rugged precipices. Rather than a few large rocks, thin layers of shale or stone placed one on top of the other to create the single precipice will provide reality. The plants should spring from the mountain stones rather than from direct planting in level areas of soil. A windswept aspect can be created by using suitable gnarled plants like *Punica granatum* or some small begonias with woody stems. A level area can complement the rock ledge but should be draped in suitable creeping plants.

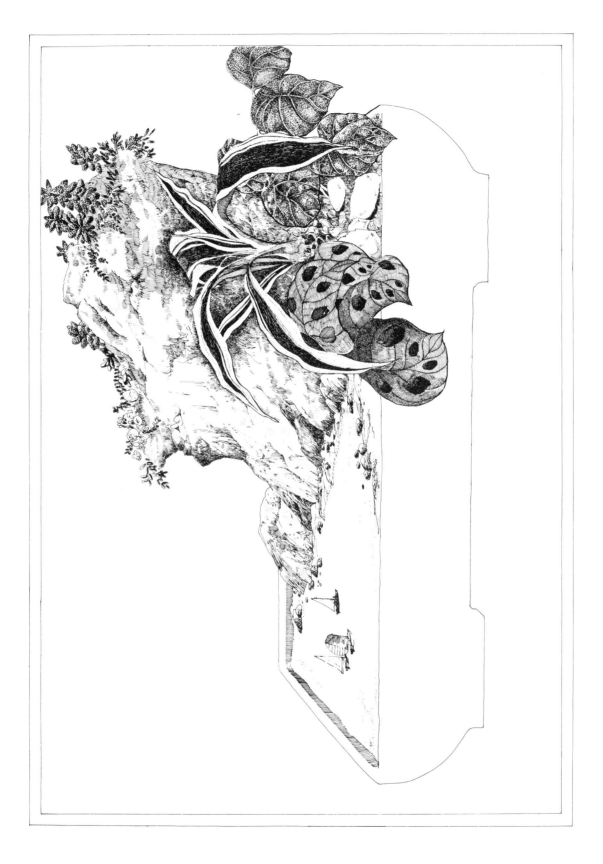

SEA COAST GARDEN

Dracaena sanderiana

Peperomia caperata

Maranta leuconeura

Sedum oaxacanum

Sedum brevifolium

Selaginella

Sedum spurium

SEA COAST GARDEN

A coastline garden requires a few choice plants rather than a jungle because its beauty relies on rock and stone formations. Even dead twigs and small limbs can be used in the landscape for reality and smaller stones in the water or sand area, with perhaps a few grasses to provide vertical accent and balance the precipice. Or use a divided tray for the garden, with the rugged coastal mountain terrain on one side and a sandy or a water area on the other. (Divided trays are available at dealers. Large trays are not necessary.)

Rocky Ledge

Like the coastline garden, the rocky ledge miniature scene should portray stark beauty. The basic ingredients are rocks and stones, with only a few well-chosen plants. The ledge should be placed to one side of the dish and be three times as high as the depth of the dish. Use osmunda to form the base, with the rocky ledges embedded in it, and then cover all with pockets of soil for the plants. The empty area to the left or to the right of the tray can be balanced with a smaller rock area, more horizontal than vertical. This area should be placed to the rear of the tray to create dimension, and the larger accent rock piece should be slightly forward.

The building of the rock ledges is more important than actual plantings. Take time and create natural precipitous formations. Once the ledge is completed, tuck plants into soil pockets where appropriate. Use coarse gravel beds around the rock formations (no soil) and pieces of decayed wood or tiny seashells to finish the scene.

Coastline Plants (Sea Coast, Rocky Ledge)

Abies balsamea var. nana. Short, flat needles tightly arranged, forming a dense ball-shaped bush.

Acer palmatum dissectum atropurpureum (red maple). Fine scalloped leaves. Makes a lovely tree.

A. p. d. viridis. Excellent lacy-leaved tree with great beauty.

Acorus graminsus variegatus. Excellent for vertical grassy effects.

Adiantum (many kinds). Ferns that add nice notes of lacy green to scene.

Araucaria excelsa (*Photo courtesy Merry Gardens*)

Araucaria excelsa (Norfolk Pine). Excellent evergreen shaped like Christmas tree. Select seedlings.

Arenaria verna caespitosa (Irish moss). Yellow-green vibrant color for quick cover.

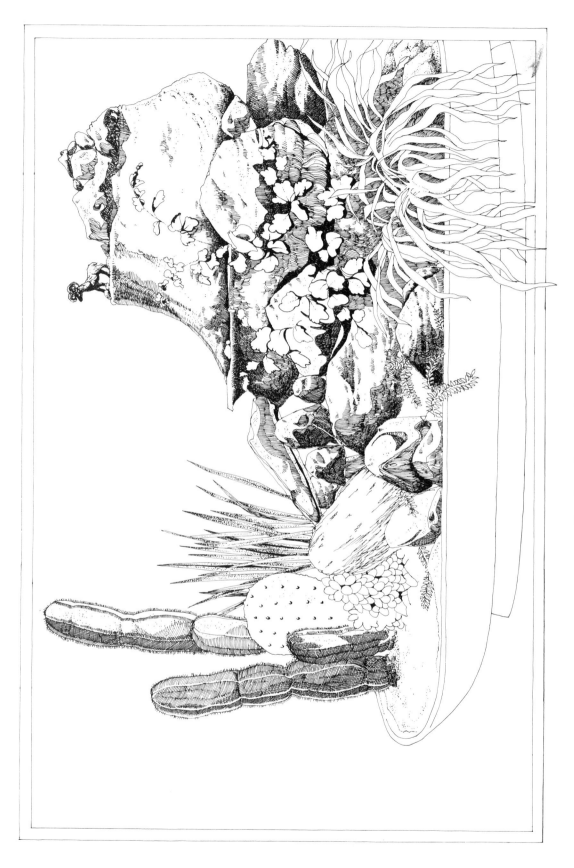

Rocky Ledge Garden

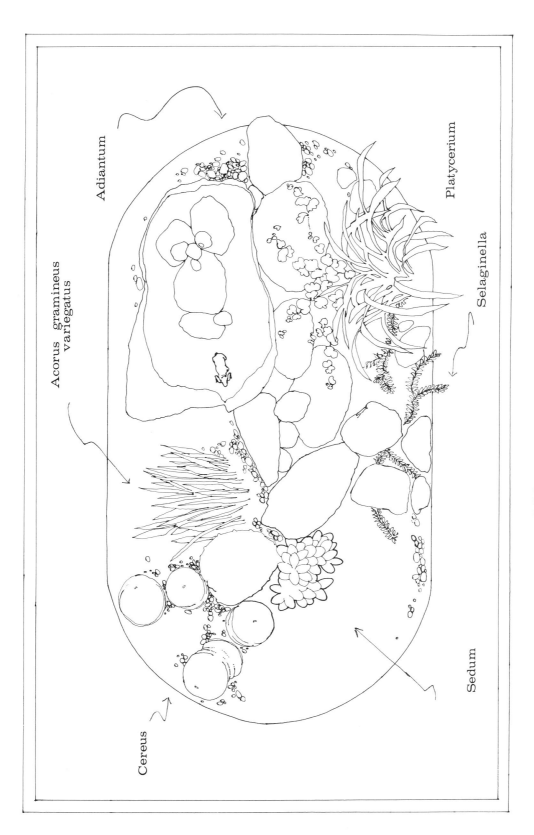

Adiantum

Platycerium

Acorus gramineus
variegatus

Selaginella

Cereus

Sedum

ROCKY LEDGE GARDEN

Asperula odorata (sweet woodruff). Grows somewhat tall, to about 8 inches. Nice vertical accent.

Buxus microphylla var. nana compacta (dwarf boxwood). Tiny leaves in tight ball.

Campanula. Many varieties. Lovely dark green leaves and bell-shaped flowers. Generally creepers; do well in coastline landscapes.

Chamaecyparis lawsoniana var. minima. Stiff fan-shaped dark green plumes; blue on undersides.

C. obtusa var. nana gracilis. Dense fan-shaped branches.

C. pisifera var. plumosa minima. Curly and feathery branchlets.

C. p. var. squarrosa aurea pygmaea. Light blue-green with golden yellow; forms a dense ball.

Crassula orbicularis. Low-growing succulent, with flat leaves in clusters.

C. radicans. Tiny-leaved; makes excellent ground cover in trays.

Cryptomeria japonica var. nana. Stiff and tiny needlelike leaves.

C. j. var. vilmoriniana. Very tiny plant, with stiff needlelike leaves.

Dracaena sanderiana. Long leaves with white borders.

Hebe decumbens. Tiny gray-green leaves; excellent for tray garden.

Helxine soleirolii (baby's tears). Tiny dark green creeper; invasive.

Juniperus chinensis var. plumosa aurea. Golden-colored vase-shaped low plant.

Maranta leuconeura (prayer plant). Good because of its beet-colored foliage.

Mentha requienii (Corsican mint). Small leaves; fine green accent for trays.

Myrsine africana (African boxwood). Charming small plant, with boxwood type growth.

Nepeta hederacea (ground ivy). Round or kidney-shaped leaves.

Oxalis. A fine group of flowering plants, with cloverlike foliage and bright colorful flowers. Tuck them between rocks for colorful accents.

Peperomia caperata. Fine dark green leaves. Excellent accent.

Picea abies var. pumila. Dense, deep dark green foliage.

Platycerium (staghorn fern). Different, and offers a unique cascading effect.

Ruellia makoyana. Erect plant with green leaves shaded red, silver veins. Lovely.

Sagina subulata (Scotch moss). Lovely dense mat of bright green.

Sedum brevifolium. Small-leaved creeping plant to cover rock work.

S. sieboldii. A good succulent, with gray-green leathery leaves. Grows easily.

S. spurium. Another low-growing larger-leaved sedum for clothing soil.

Selaginella. Tiny-leaved creeper; always good for clothing rocks.

Sempervivums. Many species. *S. arachnoideum* and its varieties are natural rock-loving plants and succeed beautifully in rock plantings. Plants are generally rosettes, some very tiny, making them ideal for tray work.

Taxus cuspidata var. minima. Tiny dark green leaves; very small plant.

Thymus (thyme). Many species; small-leaved and good creepers.

Veronica repens. Creeping mosslike plant with tiny leaves.

MOUNTAIN STREAM LANDSCAPES

This beautiful scene captures the eye and provides enjoyment. The idea is to use white sand in a graceful pattern to simulate a mountain stream between two levels of rocky formation. The accent areas can be forests, with interesting house plants placed in rocky ledges; these ledges should be of moderate height rather than very vertical as in coastline gardens. The slope should be sheer rather than gradual. Make one area dominant and the other area somewhat smaller to provide harmony. Plants should overlap the rocks and lean toward the viewer. Put in mosses lining the simulated stream, and set one accent rock formation slightly to the rear, with the other slightly to the front on the opposite side to create dimension.

Work carefully and slowly. Every detail counts, and, if something does not appear right, take it out and start again. Appropriate smaller containers of medium size can be used for this scene.

Plants used for sea coast and rocky ledge scenes are also suitable for the mountain stream landscapes (see previous section).

WOODLAND GARDENS

The lush greenness of the woodland scene attracts many people. Miniature gardens depicting these views are easy to put together. There are dozens of small houseplants, creepers and mosses, and wild plants to create a delightful green picture. Slope the soil slightly so it is somewhat hilly but never with sharp declines and peaks. A rolling terrain is what you are seeking. Start your accent island to the front or rear on one side of the tray; this can include, say, three or four plants of the same kind framed with small stones. Make this area either low and bushy or upright and graceful. Near this planting balance the scene with appropriate vertical mass or horizontal lines, depending upon the overall plan. In the center of the tray incorporate some low-growing plants surrounded by creepers and mosses, and to the left of the tray, almost covering from front to back, use another group of plants to give dimension to the landscape.

In the woodland garden (all other gardens too), use small-leaved and medium-sized plants, and a few large, bold-leaved specimens. In other words, provide constant eye interest rather than plants of all the same leaf size or color. Use dark green and light green plants—a variety rather than one solid color. However, do not put dark green plants right next to light green ones because this will jar the eye. Unify the color by using a dark green next to a medium green to a light green and the pale green (or vice versa).

The woodland scene should mound in the center of the dish or tray rather than be a solid mass from corner to corner; the design should follow an arc rather than geometrical lines. Oval or elliptical rather large trays will suit the design best.

WOODLAND GARDEN

Adiantum
tenerum

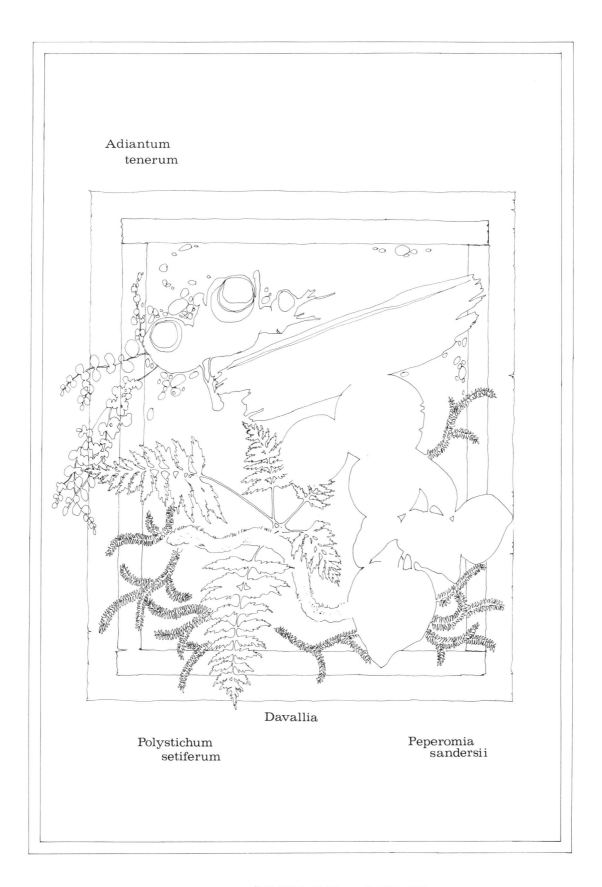

Davallia

Polystichum
setiferum

Peperomia
sandersii

WOODLAND   GARDEN

Woodland Plants (Forest Floor)

Adiantum tenerum (maidenhair fern). Small fern, with very lacy emerald green fronds. Delicate and delightful plant.

A. splenium platyneuron (ebony spleenwort). Feathery fronds and brown-purple stems. Large but good.

A. trichomanes (maidenhair spleenwort). A 6-inch fern, with clustered fronds and 1-inch leaflets on black stems.

Chimaphila maculata (striped pipsissewa). Arrow-shaped leaves with lovely veining.

Coptis trifolia (goldthread). A dainty plant, with handsome scalloped leaves.

Cyperus alternifolius. Graceful grassy leaves on tall stems.

Cyperus (*Photo courtesy Merry Gardens*)

76

Plectranthus (*Photo courtesy Merry Gardens*)

Cypripedium acaule (pink ladyslipper). Pink and lovely, but needs a strongly acid soil.

C. pubescens. Yellow flowers; large grower.

Davallia bullata mariesii (rabbit's foot fern). Creeping brown rhizomes, lacy fronds. Select small plants; can grow large.

Dionaea rotundifolia (Venus flytrap). Curious insect-eating plant. Small, with bright green claw foliage. An oddity.

Drosera rotundifolia (sundew). Unique plant that is fascinating to watch. Tiny round leaves with hairy blades that capture insects.

Epigaea repens (trailing arbutus). Bright green leaves and white or pink flowers. Needs a very acid soil to survive.

77

Hepatica acutiloba (sharp-leaved liverleaf). Three-lobed leaves; flowers may be white or pink. Grows in neutral soil, and probably will be the first in the dish garden to bloom.

Humata tyermannii. Small and delicate; very lacy fronds. Excellent.

Microlepia setosa. Tiny delicate fern, with feathery fronds.

Mitchella repens (partridge berry). Evergreen creeper that bears red berries at Christmas and lasts for many weeks.

Pellaea rotundifolia (button fern). Tiny button leaves of dark green on wiry stems.

Peperomia sandersii. Small-leaved, good color. Branching.

Polystichum setisforum. Lacy fern with nice branching habit.

Pyrola elliptica (wintergreen). A 3-inch leaved plant, with white flowers.

Trillium grandiflorum. Bears lovely white flowers with pink hues and grows to 18 inches.

DESERT GARDENS

The desert garden's austere, simple beauty is challenging. Its beauty depends upon a sparse planting and a keen eye to detail. It is what is *not* in the garden rather than what is in it that makes this an artistic achievement. Also, plants for this garden (cacti and succulents) must be carefully selected because not all cacti are desert dwellers—some like rain-forest conditions—and because the succulent family is so vast, choosing the right plants is sometimes confusing.

Hills and valleys may be part of the desert scene, but basically this is almost a flat terrain, with rock ledges and small stone formations. Unlike other gardens, where groups of the same plant can be used, the desert garden needs one large accent plant and then smaller plants placed strategically in the tray. The arc arrangement works well here, and color of the plants is important because cacti and succulents come in many colors, from bright apple green to dark blue-green. Cacti shapes are barrel, globular, candelabra, and columnar; in succulents the choice involves many thick-leaved, generally oval-leaved, plants in varying colors, from gray to apple green rosettes. Thus, shapes of plants and how one is used to complement the other is the key to an attractive desert tray landscape.

When planting the desert garden, remember that soil, *not* sand, will be needed for plant roots, so individual pockets of soil must be incorporated into the landscape. Build rockwork carefully and precisely so it appears to be part of the landscape rather than just tucked in as an afterthought (see Chapter 5). Use a rather large tray to establish reality.

Desert Plants

Adromischus clavifolius. Small, with club-shaped leaves flecked with reddish marks.

A. maculatus (calico hearts). Thick gray-green leaves spotted with brown.

Aloe brevifolia variegata. Beautiful vertically striped leaves laced with lines of white.

Astrophytum myriostigma (bishop's cap). Spineless plant shaped like a bishop's hood.

Cereus (many kinds). Columnar and good upright accent.

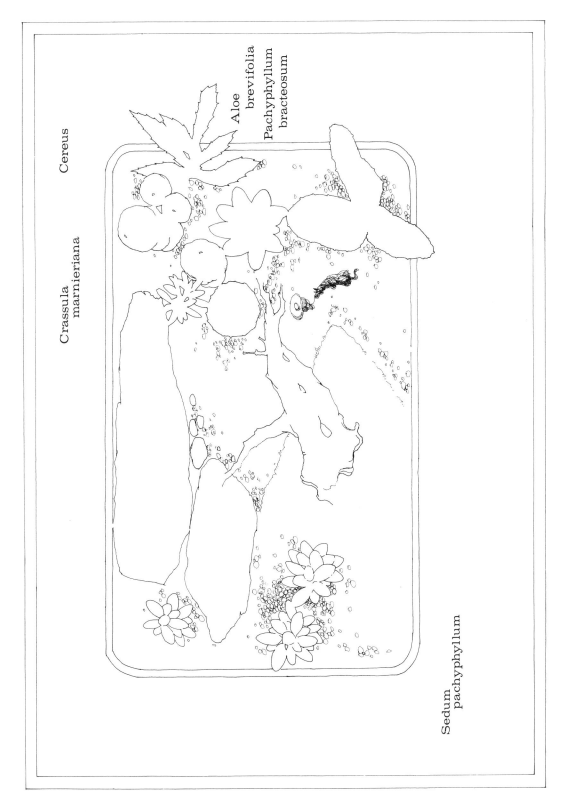

Cereus

Crassula
marnieriana

Aloe
brevifolia
Pachyphyllum
bracteosum

Sedum
pachyphyllum

DESERT GARDEN

Cleistocactus straussii. Spiny columnar cacti of grayish green.

Cotyledon. A group of succulent plants. Leaves are leathery and light or dark green.

Crassula cooperi. Three-inch leathery-leaved plant.

C. marmieriana. Fine small-leaved succulent; good upright accent.

Lobivias (*Photo by Joyce R. Wilson*)

C. schmidtii. Handsome plant, with red tinted leaves.

Euphorbia obesa (basketball plant). A perfectly round gray-green globe with purple seams. An oddity but excellent.

Gasteria liliputanta. Thick stubby dark green leaves in a spiral pattern; mottled pale green.

Gymnocalycium mihanovichii (chin cactus). Brightly colored green plant with ribbed formation.

Haworthia fasciata (zebra haworthia). Dark green leaves banded crosswise with rows of white dots.

H. tessellata. Starlike rosette with dark green leaves lined with pale green.

Lobivia. Many fine small cactus—olive-green to gray.

Myrtillocactus cochal. Spiny and bizarre branched cacti.

Pachyphytum bracteosum. Good small cacti for gray-green color accent.

Rebutia kupperiana. Small gray-green globe; stays tiny.

Sedums. A large group of plants with many small species. Try *S. rubrotinctum, S. lineare, S. confusum, S. pachyphyllum.*

TROPICAL LANDSCAPES

A tropical landscape is a favorite lilliputian garden because you can use so many favorite houseplants and get a lush and verdant effect. Put in many plants, with one plant flowing into the next so a rich green

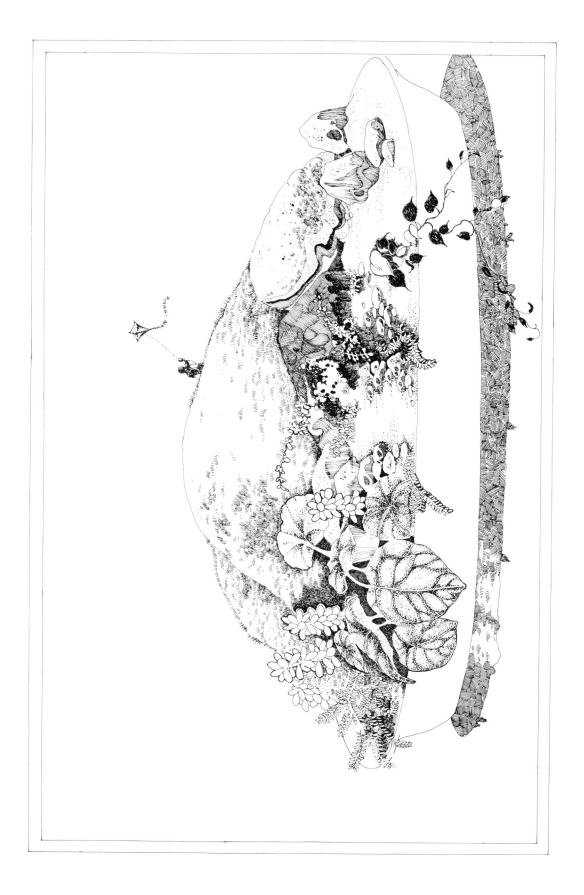

TROPICAL GARDEN

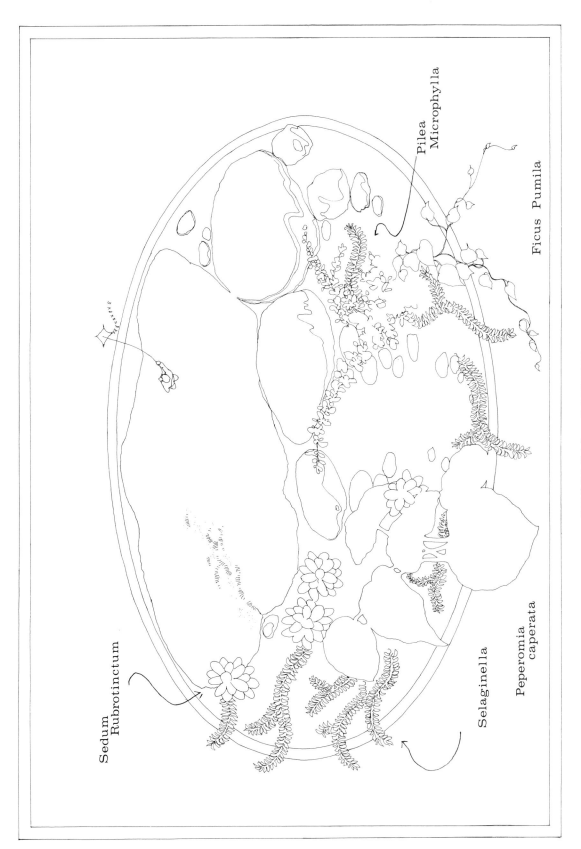

Sedum
Rubrotinctum

Pilea
Microphylla

Ficus Pumila

Selaginella

Peperomia
caperata

TROPICAL GARDEN

color prevails. Make one area higher than the rest of the landscape, and use creeping ground covers to clothe the soil with green. Concentrate on vertical growers rather than branching plants so there is not a tangled jungle effect. You need good eye interest here to create an attractive piece, and vertical thrust helps greatly.

Make the soil contour slightly hilly. To create reality, use interesting small pieces of wood and bark; stones and rocks should *not* be in this landscape. Select plants which prefer somewhat moist conditions at all times and avoid plants, such as succulents, which will rot with overwatering. Dark green plants should predominate, with perhaps some lighter green ones, but basically this is a purely green-green garden with occasional flashes of bright color. Flowering plants will supply the colorful blossoms (there are many to choose from). Each group of plants should be an entity in itself and yet relate to other groups. Harmony in design is essential to avoid a cluttered look. The tropical landscape is best fashioned in a large tray.

Tropical Plants

Aglaonema commutatum (Chinese evergreen). Dark green leaves with silver markings.

Anthurium scherzerianum (flamingo plant). Attractive green leaves, shiny red bracts.

Ascocentrum miniatum. Orchid, with tiny bright orange flowers.

Azalea 'Gumpo.' Delightful small azalea, with frilly red flowers. Good tree accent.

Bambusa nana (miniature bamboo). Grassy plant, with graceful pale green leaves.

Begonias. A vast group of miniatures are available in this family, and many have interesting treelike growth, making them perfect subjects. Consult catalogs for best ones.

Begonia "Lulandi" (above)
(Photo courtesy Joyce R.
Wilson) Begonia "Specu-
lata" (left) Photo by Joyce
R. Wilson)

Broughtonia sanguinea. Solitary green leaves; lovely brick red flowers.

Caladiums. Many fine varieties, with heart-shaped colorful leaves. Try *C. humboldtii* "Little Rascal" or *C. h.* "Twilight."

Group of Calatheas (*Photo courtesy Alberts & Merkel*)

Calathea bachemiana. Velvety gray-green leaves.

Chamaedorea elegans (bamboo plant). Lovely dwarf palm, with bright green fronds.

Chamaeranthemum igneum. Tropical creeper, with velvety bronze-brown leaves and pink veins.

Codiaeum variegatum pictum (croton). Branching plant with woody stem; makes excellent small tree. Colorful foliage. Many varieties.

Crossandra infundibuliformis (orange glory). Fine shiny green leaves; orange flowers.

Cryptanthus bivittatus (rosea picta). Bronze-pink foliage striped pale green.

C. bromeliodes tricolor. A rosette of green leaves striped pink and white.

Ctenanthe oppenheimiana. Dark green foliage with silver markings.

Dizygotheca elegantissima (false aralia). Lovely scalloped leaves; woody stems. Makes good tree.

Dracaena godseffiana. Small-growing, yellow and green leaves.

Episcia dianthiflora. Velvety leaves of intense green. Small and dainty.

Ficus pumila (creeping fig). Fine tiny plant with button-shaped leaves.

Hypocyrta nummularia (goldfish plant). Shiny small green leaves; pretty orange flowers.

Impatiens. Look for dwarf varieties ('Red Elfin') with bright red flowers.

Kalanchoe blossfeldiana. Many varieties; seek small ones. Red or orange flowers.

Malpighia coccigera (miniature holly). Glossy green leaves on branching stems. A good tree-type specimen.

Maranta leuconeura kerchoveana (prayer plant). One of the most beautiful foliage plants, with iridescent leaf markings.

Nerium oleander. Branching plants, with dark green lancelike leaves. Nice accent for trays.

Oncidium pumilum. Small dark green leaves; yellow flowers. Nice low-growing orchid.

Ornithocephalus grandiflorus. Fleshy green leaves; pale green flowers.

Oxalis. A fine group of flowering plants. Try *O. hedysaroides*, with golden flowers, or *O. henrei*, with tiny yellow blooms.

Pandanus veitchii (corkscrew plant). Striped yellow and green leaves. Rosette growth; makes a nice small "palm."

Peperomias. A large group of excellent dish and tray plants. Leaf colors vary from green to browns to maroons and variegated.

Philodendron andreanum. Nice leaf, small plant with good color.

Pilea. A vast group of small plants with colorful foliage. Leaf coloring varies from dark green to brownish green with silver markings.

Polyscias fruticosa elegans (ming tree). A delightful tray plant which looks like a ming tree. Lacy green foliage and fine branching habit.

Punica granatum nana (dwarf pomegranate). Lovely small-leaved tree. Look for P. 'Chico.'

Rosa (Rose). Dozens of varieties of charming plants.

Philodendron andreanum (*left*) (*Photo courtesy Merry Gardens*) St. Augustine grass (*right*) (*Photo courtesy Merry Gardens*)

Sansevieria hahni. A spiral of dark broad green leaves. S. 'Golden Hahni' excels with green and yellow leaves.

Stenotaphrum secundatum variegatum (St. Augustine grass). Green and white leaves, trailing plant.

LAKE SCENES

Years ago my grandmother used to make this scene with small mirrors as the lake area. Basically the same planting as for a hillside garden can be done, with the lake the focal point. Place the "water" forward to the left or right on the tray but never directly in the center. To be natural the design should have the lake framed with plants and the contour of the landscape must be gracefully executed in gradual incline. Try to maintain a slight incline as plant material moves away from the lake. Abrupt changes in height should be avoided because this creates a spotty effect.

The lake is the dominant part of the garden, but you will need other accents to balance the scene, so rock ledges of wooded formations to left or right of the water area are suitable. Although the lake can be a small mirror, you can also use white sand, as is done in sakei landscapes. The lake may be framed by hills (but only on one side), or the hills may be somewhat removed from the lake. Use sand around the lake to create a natural effect. A mirror merely framed with plants will look unreal, but some gravel chips and sand at the edges of the area will lend an authentic note to lead to hills and plants. Use some grasses and standard houseplants rather than mosses as lush vegetation.

Lake Scene Plants

Acorus gramineus variegatus. Tufted lovely grassy plant which does well in moist situations.

Adiantum tenerum (maidenhair fern). Lacy leaved deep green fern. Graceful and arching.

Bambusa (bamboo). Many fine small species with feathery leaves.

Cordyline terminalis (ti-plant). Fine rosette plant with dark green leaves edged red.

Dieffenbachia amoena. Variegated plant with single trunk.

Peperomia glomerata. A good peperomia which likes saturated soil.

Philodendron cordatum. Can grow in very moist conditions.

Pothos. Heart-shaped shiny green leaves. Trailer.

92

Group of Dieffenbachias (*Photo courtesy Merry Gardens*)

Syngonium podophyllum (arrowhead). Leafy plant with tall stems and arrow-shaped leaves.

Tolmiea menziesii (piggyback plant). Bushy and full with light green leaves.

Tradescantia fluminensis (wandering jew). Grows like a weed and has oval-shaped leaves.

HILLSIDE GARDENS & MEADOW GARDENS

A hilly terrain always pleases the eye. These small gardens need many plants. However, you want a constant flow of plant material with

93

some bare areas here and there to establish a point of reference rather than a jungle. Some of the hills may be bare on top, with plants framing the peaks. To create the hilly contour, use pieces of rock covered with soil. Some rock can be visible, but I find the completely clothed hillside miniature the most pleasing.

The terrain will be more important here than in any other garden, so do this building first before you put in a single plant. Create flowing lines to a center valley, and shape and detail each hill so it is in pleasing relationship to the other hill. Use somewhat large containers, say 16 by 24 inches, to really establish a sense of reality. Small handcrafted bridges and little houses can be fitting accompaniments to the hillside garden, and gravel and sand areas can be used with discretion.

Hillside and Meadow Garden Plants

Acorus gramineus variegatus. Handsome grassy plant. Small, good.

Bambusa nana (bamboo). Lovely dainty leaves of apple green; gives grassy feeling to garden.

Begonia boweri (eyelash begonia). Fine small begonia with chartreuse leaves stitched black.

B. dregei. Looks like small tree. Excellent choice.

B. rotundifolia. Round shiny leaves; compact and bushy accent.

Calathea. Generally small dark green-leaved plants. Many kinds.

Chlorophytum comosum (spider plant). Arching and graceful with thin grassy yellow and green foliage.

Cryptanthus. Small star-shaped bromeliads in many varieties; excellent color.

94

Osmanthus variegatus (holly) (*Photo courtesy Merry Garden*)

Helxine soleirolii (baby's tears). Grows fast but very effective with small round dark green leaves.

Maranta. Some lovely small variegated plants; very colorful.

Peperomia caperata. Popular peperomia with heart-shaped leaves, apple green.

Philodendron. Choose small-leaved species; mostly vining plants.

Pteris cretica. Lovely fern with arching stems. Many varieties.

Sagina (Scotch moss). Yellow-green grassy plant which makes a fine effect in small gardens.

MEADOW GARDEN

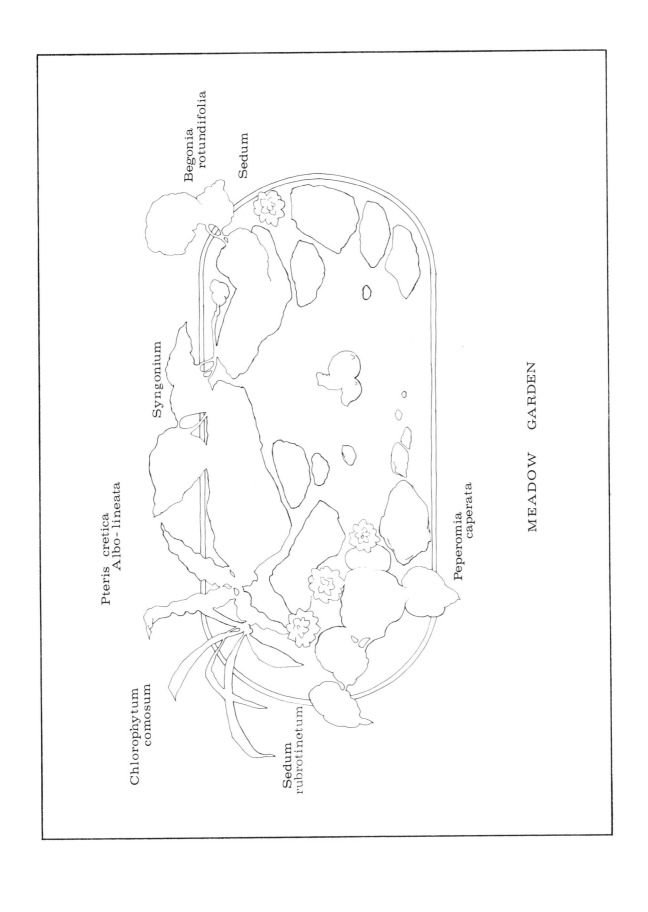

Begonia
rotundifolia

Sedum

Syngonium

Pteris cretica
Albo-lineata

Chlorophytum
comosum

Sedum
rubrotinctum

Peperomia
caperata

MEADOW GARDEN

Saintpaulia (African violet). Miniature varieties are lovely indeed and come in flower colors of white or pink.

Sedum rubrotinctum. Nice small-leaved sedum.

Selaginella. Low creepers of emerald green. Many species.

Syngonium podophyllum (arrowhead). Tall stems with arrow-shaped leaves. Fast grower.

SINGLE ROCK GARDENS

This lilliputian landscape depends on simplicity for its beauty. The rock takes center stage here with a few small pebbles as a balance and the plants are sparse—purposely so. Each plant should be carefully selected for beauty and grace and while grass may be present in the landscape, sprawling ground covers should be omitted.

The rock should be placed at one corner of the container—generally the rear; around it the few plants grouped in a semicircle. A somewhat large plant, perhaps a begonia, can be used at the opposite corner of the tray to create dimension in the landscape. Other plants should be purposely small so as not to steal the show.

A deep container, say 4 to 5 inches, is best for the single rock scene because the depth again is in proportion to the height of the rock. When anchoring the rock be sure it appears as part of the total landscape; it should be partially buried with the top prominent.

Various kinds of plants can be used in this type of garden with the exception of cacti, which would be out of place against a rocky terrain—somewhat reminiscent of sea coast greeneries.

The single rock garden landscape is easy to arrange and provides stark beauty rather than a lush effect. It definitely has its uses as a decorative piece for the home.

Plants

Acorus gramineus. Simple grassy plant with well-defined leaves.

Bambusa (bamboo). Use the small-leaved species and keep them trimmed. Dainty and lovely.

Begonia boweri (stitch-leaf begonia). A handsome plant with chartreuse leaves stitched in black. Outstanding.

Buxus microphylla var. nana compacta (dwarf boxwood). A fine small boxwood with tiny leaves in a tight ball.

Broughtonia sanguinea. Solitary green leaves; small, with lovely red flowers.

Cryptanthus. Any of these would be fine for the single rock garden; excellent color.

Davallia. Many fine small graceful ferns in this group and the majority are lovely. Lacy and dainty.

Malpighia coccigera (miniature holly). Glossy green leaves and branching stems. Good tree-type accent.

Oncidium pumilum. Small dark green leaves; yellow flowers. Low-growing orchid.

Oncidium rogersi. Small dark green leaves and fine pink flowers.

Polyscias fruticosa elegans (ming tree). Fine treelike plant with scalloped leaves. Graceful.

Punica granatum nana (dwarf pomegranate). Lovely small tree with tiny leaves. Good accent.

Syngonium podophyllum (arrowhead). Not stellar but nice arrow-shaped leaves on tall stems.

Single Rock Garden

Davallia

Begonia
boweri

Oncidium
rogersi

SINGLE ROCK GARDEN

7 GROW YOUR OWN plants

You can of course buy plants for the various gardens you want to make, but often you must take what is available rather than what you want. Also, there is the element of cost: model landscapes and tray gardens take more plants than you might think to make them attractive, and this can run into money. So it is the wise gardener who decides to grow some plants of his own; nature is very free with gifts, and everyone likes something for nothing. And there is great satisfaction in rearing a tiny seedling into a full-grown plant. Like children, your own are your best.

Above: Sphagnum is an excellent starting medium for seeds. (*Photo by Jack Barnick*) *Right*: a shallow casserole can be used for seed-sowing. (*Photos by author*)

What generally confuses the average gardener is the many ways to get new plants from old ones or the many methods of starting seeds and cuttings. You can get new plants by sowing seed (inexpensive), taking leaf cuttings, from tiny plants that appear at the base of some plants, or by simply dividing a plant. Technical terms can frighten the would-be gardener, yet propagating plants is quite simple, as we shall show you.

WHAT YOU WILL NEED

To grow your own plants you will need some kind of container: a standard clay pot, a discarded casserole dish or aluminum packages frozen rolls come in, or any other kind of container which is at least

103

4 to 5 inches deep. Whatever you use, be sure it has some small drainage holes in the bottom.

You will also need a rooting medium; use the packaged "starters" sold at nurseries. These starters include vermiculite, perlite, or combinations of inert materials. Any medium that is sterile can be used, even sand. Small plants and seed need good humidity to start growth, so devise a tent structure to keep moisture in the medium. Put small sticks upright in the medium, and then simply drape a Baggie or any flexible plastic over the sticks. Find a bright and warm (75°F) place for the propagating box; I find the top of the refrigerator a fine spot. It is also a good idea to have a small jar of hormone rooting powder (at nurseries) for cuttings.

HOW TO PROPAGATE PLANTS

A cutting (slip) is merely part of the tip of the stem; cut off a piece 3 or 4 inches in length. Make cuttings during a plant's natural growth time: spring or early summer (it just will not work well in other seasons). Leave the tip leaves and discard the rest.

You can try rooting the cutting in water, but ideally you must grow slips in a growing medium. Dip the cut end of the slip in rooting hormone, and then insert the cutting into the growing medium (vermiculite, sand, and so on). Water the medium but do not drench it. Make sure there is ample space between cuttings. Now cover the cuttings with the "tent" we mentioned in the previous section, and place the cuttings in a warm (75°F) shady place.

After several weeks roots will have formed. You can now remove the tent and put the new plant in a 3-inch pot of soil. Keep the potted plants in a bright, but not sunny, reasonably warm place until you are ready to use them in dish landscapes.

104

Leaf Cuttings

Taking leaf cuttings from many succulents and gesneriads is an incredibly easy way to propagate plants. Cut leaves with a sterile razor blade, and dip the severed ends in rooting hormone. Then insert the leaves in vermiculite or sand, with leaves half in and half out of the medium.

Plants like Sansevieria can be propagated by slicing a leaf in 2-inch sections, as you would a sausage. To multiply, say, Rex begonias, make several cuts at the junctions of the veins in the leaves. Pin down the leaf in moist medium (such as vermiculite) so the cut area is in contact with the medium. New plants will appear at these junctions. When the plants are about 1 to 2 inches tall they can be potted in-dividually in soil. In a few more weeks they will be ready to transplant into your dish gardens. (Some people skip the last transplanting and move the seedlings directly from the propagating medium into small gardens.)

Here, cuttings are put into plastic bag to insure humidity. (*Photo by USDA*)

Tip cuttings are easy to take and then are placed in starting medium. (*Photo by USDA*)

Offshoots and Division

An offshoot is the very tiny plant you will see that sprouts from the base of the mother plant. Plants such as Agaves, Begonias, Orchids, and Bromeliads all produce offshoots and these little babies can—when they are 3 to 4 inches high—be removed from the parent plant and started in soil or vermiculite. Keep them warm (about 75°F) and in bright light.

When they have regained vigor and are starting to grow (about a month depending on the type of plant) they can be moved to add beauty to your miniature garden.

Division is pulling apart a plant with crowns and then using each section separately to get new plants. It—like offshoots—is an easy way to get new little plants for your gardens without any cost.

While many people find it difficult to know when a plant is old enough to divide, there is one simple way: look directly down at a rosette-type growth plant such as a fern. You will be able to see the divisions (clumps). Pull these clumps apart gently, or cut them with a sharp knife. They can now be potted in soil to grow on for a month or so or you can if you want (and I do) place them directly into soil in the miniature garden.

Both division and offshoots are very easy ways to dress up a miniature garden quickly and more than once I have clipped off an offshoot or pulled up a division from a mature plant to use when I want the garden especially pretty if, say, guests are coming.

Seeds are sown in peat pots for germination; some seedlings are already up. (*Photo by author*)

Growing Plants From Seed

This process of acquiring new plants is relatively easy but it does take time. In many cases, it will be several months before plants will be suitable for your small gardens. Still, sowing seed has other rewards besides being inexpensive. There is the satisfaction of growing your very own plants and this gives one a good feeling.

Use any container that is at least 4 inches deep and one you can put drain holes in so excess water can escape. Shallow clay pots, aluminum food cartons, even cottage cheese cartons or a milk carton cut in half lengthwise will be suitable for seeds. Insert a 3-inch layer of growing medium—vermiculite, sand, or any packaged starter—in the container. Scatter small seeds on top of the medium and larger seeds will have to be embedded their girth.

To germinate (start growth), most seeds need warmth (about 75° to 78°F), so place the container and seeds in a warm spot. I find the top of my refrigerator a fine place. Seeds do not need bright light; indeed it could kill them. Keep the seed bed moist by misting it; use a spray bottle with water and mist medium gently. If the seeds get too dry they will die, too wet and they will develop a disease called damping-off (which is just about being next to death). Keep a Baggie on sticks over the container, but never allow it to get too moist inside. If the inside gets too clouded with condensed moisture, remove the Baggie a few hours a day.

When you see signs of new growth, add a very weak plant food solution (5-5-5) once a week. Pot seedlings in separate containers when they are about 3 inches high or you can move them directly to the dish garden to grow on.

You get lots of seeds for little money and because there are so many the odds that you will be successful are all in your favor. It is possible to plant seeds (of different houseplants) about every three months and always have a fresh supply of tiny plants for your gardens. And at little cost!

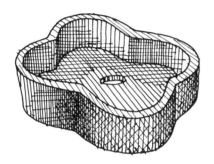

8 small gardens for small kids

Many times it is difficult to get children interested in gardening. A plant in a pot at the window grows too slowly for anxious youngsters, and there is very little they can do to get their hands into things with a window plant. Watering it every day can become more of a chore than a pleasure. Few kids like to follow daily regimes. So if you want a surprise and to see your kids really get interested in gardening, have them try miniature gardens. Here they are working with their hands and minds and those little fingers can create some unusual arrangements.

HOW TO GET THEM STARTED

To start, give children an inexpensive small tray and only a few plants and soil and stones. You might set up the garden by putting in drainage material and gravel, but from then on let the child do it and don't interfere no matter how grotesquely the arrangement may develop. After placing a few plants and seeing the garden a few days, young minds will naturally realize mistakes and then they will move plants about until they get it to their liking (not yours).

Many of the seedlings from your mature plants can be used for your offspring's gardens. Plants such as small Philodendrons, Ferns, peperomias, and miniature species will do fine. Encourage children to create a scene they have recently visited—perhaps the park or the inside of a conservatory. Supply some tiny figurines (these are inexpensive) for young fingers to work with, call by name perhaps, and include a few props like little bridges or tiny boathouses. Better yet, if your child is handy let him make the props himself from small pieces of wood or matchsticks. Get the imagination going and in no time you will find an eager young mind will take over.

PATHS, WALKS, AND SO FORTH

Show kids the beauty of stones and pebbles and sand; let them collect them—seashells too and odd bits of driftwood—for their gardens. At first you might have to build a rocky ledge but then let the child do it. If the youngster comes home with a snail or frog for the garden you are in trouble, but it is as good a time as any to explain that some insects are good, others bad. The snail (not really an insect) will eat good plants while the frog will eat bad little insects. (And now you will have a frog

Children's tray gardens can be simple as shown here with a small bamboo and ground cover. (*Photo by author*)

hopping around the house.) So another lesson is in order, but it all adds to education and eventually to having a youngster create his own miniature garden that he or she will be proud of and observe daily. And what a way to keep kids busy when it is raining outdoors!

SOME EASY PLANTS

There is little question that some plants grow easier than others; they can tolerate untenable situations if necessary and still thrive. These are the plants for the kids' gardens. Instant failure of a plant will result in a child's instant abandonment of the landscape so provide robust plants. These include a host of varieties you can buy in 2-inch pots at

Tiny plants in a plastic container can be used to create a children's dish garden. (*Photo by author*)

nurseries. For example, the prayer plant (Maranta) is always fascinating with its colored foliage. The aluminum plant (*Pilea cadieri minima*) grows like a weed and the small selaginellas and mosses cover soil quickly. The spider plant (Chlorophytum) is another good candidate for youngsters' gardens: so is the piggy-back plant (Tolmiea) and the strawberry geranium (*Saxifraga sarmentosa*) that produces tiny babies on runner-type stems. These will keep the young interested and asking questions!

If all this fails to intrigue, there are always carnivorous plants. Venus flytrap (*Dionaea muscipula*) and the Sundew plant (*Drosera rotundifolia*) have a special fascination for kids. These plants are now at many local nurseries and are perfect for gardens because they are naturally small. Don't expect them to live too long because they do need high humidity and utmost care, but with careful tending they will last about a year, which is a longer time than most toys last.

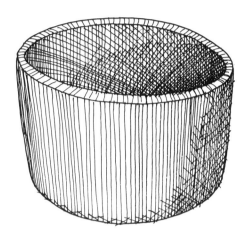

9 care of miniature Gardens

Once you have made your tray landscape you will want to keep it beautiful. It is a work of art, not just a mere conglomeration of plants, and as such you will want to care for it to have it for years instead of months.

The care of tray landscapes differs from growing plants in pots at windowsills. Water simply cannot be dumped into a tray as can be done with potted plants. Pruning and trimming are essential, and the elements of all good plant growth—air, humidity, moisture, and light—are vital.

PLACEMENT, WATERING, AND FEEDING

Your tray landscape can occupy any place in the home where there is bright light. In winter some sun is fine. Thus the landscape can be on a table or desk, at a window, or in a special niche of its own in a living room. If you are not satisfied with it in one area, move it elsewhere. But generally the miniature garden should be used as a decorative accessory to a room rather than just as a potted plant. Well-done landscapes can enhance a room with great beauty and should be used this way.

Different plants will need different watering, but usually the soil should be moistened thoroughly twice a week (water running out of the drain holes). Use a spout watering can and apply a *gentle* stream of water so as not to dislodge soil or sand. Many plants object to icy water, so for best results allow water to stand in a watering can overnight before using it the following day (the best time to water plants is in early morning or early evening). Soil should always be evenly moist (except for desert gardens) and never soggy. Because rock plantings are very liable to get dry, they will need frequent careful watering.

You will also need a mister to moisten plants and arrangements about once a week and to provide some additional humidity. In warm weather spray plants with water every day to keep them fresh.

Because you want your plants to stay small, there is no need to feed them; if soil is replenished periodically (say every 18 months), plants will have sufficient nutrients and require no additional feeding. Indeed, fertilizing plants can do them more harm than good. However, if you think you must feed plants, do it only when they are in active growth, generally in spring or summer, and not at all the rest of the year. Be sure the soil is moistened before you do feeding, and never feed ailing or sick plants to bring them back to life because this is sure death. For most plants a general all-purpose soluble plant food (10-10-5) can be used.

Good air circulation is needed by all plants, including those in decorative gardens. See that they have a free movement of air, especially during the winter when days are dark and gloomy. With less moisture in winter, when most plants rest, red spider mite may attack plants unless there is ample air circulation. Average home temperatures of 68° to 75°F during the day and 10° less at night will suit most plants in small gardens. The difference between night and day temperatures is necessary for good plant growth because plants assimilate foods better at night with cooler temperatures than if in warmth.

Humidity, as mentioned, can be supplied by spraying leaves with water every other day or so. However, because many plants are growing together, they themselves will help to create additional humidity if your rooms are warm. But, if you want to be very sure about humidity, set containers within containers on a bed of pea gravel kept moist. You can also have special galvanized tray containers made at sheet-metal shops to use as a base for the tray landscape; set the tray on this.

HEALTH TIPS

Plants, like people, are prone to ailments or may not respond in certain conditions. Here are some things to watch for:

- Avoid sudden changes of temperature; this can shock plants and cause leaf drop. Gradual changes of temperature are fine.

- Always keep plants out of drafts, but be sure they have good air circulation.

- Strong sunlight can many times scorch leaves; bright light is best (east or west window).

- Too much water can cause root damage, so use discretion when watering.

CRAWLY THINGS

If all cultural conditions are good and plants still drop leaves or leaves turn brown or yellow, be on the alert for insect damage. Generally a healthy plant will not attract insects, but there is always a time when insects may get a foothold. If they do, do not panic because there are ways to get rid of them without too much trouble.

The main consideration in keeping plants insect-free is to observe them daily; then, if you see a few insects, it is simple to get rid of them. The most common insects to attack plants are mealybugs, aphids, scale, thrips, and red spider.

Most of these pests can be eliminated with common household remedies. A mixture of laundry soap and water touched on the insect (with a cotton swab) will help deter mealybugs, aphids, and scale.

This miniature garden is crowded and plants need to be trimmed and pruned so scale and balance are achieved. (*Photo by author*)

Repeat applications every other day, and always rinse plants thoroughly with plain water afterward. Alcohol on a cotton swab will also eliminate many plant pests, and boiling water poured on soil will thwart thrips.

If the old-fashioned remedies are too time-consuming and you want quick remedies, you must resort to pesticides. (Generally the smell of pesticides is enough not to use them, let alone the aspect of having poisons in the home.) But a small aerosol houseplant spray is all right to use on plants provided you spray them in a well-ventilated area and away from the kitchen. Also keep all chemicals out of reach of children and pets. Check the label on the package to be sure it will kill the pests you are fighting. Some sprays only deter aphids, and others may kill both mealybugs and aphids, so it is wise to read the fine print and always follow directions to the letter.

GROOMING

This section may seem superfluous, but if you want healthy plants without insects or diseases, you will have to remove dead leaves and stems from model landscapes whenever you see them because once they return to the soil they can help to contribute to plant diseases. Sanitation is simply good common sense, so keep soil free of debris and all plants in tiptop shape.

Do not be afraid to shape and trim plants to the desired shapes you have in mind; it does not hurt the plants, and many times it encourages new healthy growth.

Occasionally wipe the leaves with a damp cloth, and keep the container clean too. The whole composition—plants, soil, container—should be perfect in every detail because gardens are always on display and will always cause comments from guests. Keep them looking beautiful all the time so you and your friends can enjoy the beauty of nature at its best in small landscapes.

Left: A closeup showing a crowded situation with too many plants in the garden. Some judicious pruning is in order. *Below*: This woodland scene is overly crowded with plants and still looks good; eventually, however, some trimming and pruning of plants will be necessary. (*Photos by author*)

BOOKS tO REAδ

All About Miniature Plants and Gardens, Bernice Brilmayer, Doubleday & Co., 1963

Bottle Gardens and Fern Cases, Anne Ashberry, Hodder & Stoughton, 1964

Cacti as Decorative Plants, Jack Kramer, Charles Scribner's Sons, 1974

A Garden in Your House, (Rev. Ed.), Ernesta Drinker Ballard, Harper & Row, 1972

Orchids for Your Home, Jack Kramer, Cornerstone Library, 1974

Plants That Really Bloom Indoors, Ginny and George Elbert, Simon & Schuster, 1974

Miniature Flower Arrangements and Plantings, Lois Wilson, Hawthorn Books, Inc., 1963

The Complete Book of Terrarium Gardening, Jack Kramer, Charles Scribner's Sons, 1974

supplies

Containers for miniature gardens are at nurseries and plant stores and come in all sizes, shapes and designs; packaged soil is also available. Osmunda can be found at mail order orchid suppliers; it is generally available in hobby sacks. Garden departments of large stores usually have containers and soil, Woolworth's and similar stores also carry a complete line of dishes, trays and containers for miniature gardens as well as accessories such as figurines and so forth.

where to buy plants

Alberts & Merkel Bros., Inc.
2210 S. Federal Hwy.
Boynton Beach, Fla. 33435

Arthur Eames Allgrove
Box 459
Wilmington, Mass. 01887

Barrington Greenhouse
860 Clemente Rd.
Barrington, N.J. 08016

Cactus by Mueller
10411 Rosedale Hwy.
Bakersfield, Calif. 93307

Cook's Geranium Nursery
712 N. Grand
Lyons, Kansas 67554

Henrietta's Cactus Nursery
1345 N. Brawley
Fresno, Calif. 93705

Ilgenfritz, Margaret, Orchids
Monroe, Michigan 48161

Logee's Greenhouses
55 North Street
Danielson, Conn. 06239

Merry Gardens
Camden, Maine 04843

The above mail order suppliers carry miniature plants; most have catalogs and charge for them. Charges vary from .50 to $2 and generally the price of the catalog is refundable upon receipt of order of plants.